90 Days to Write Your Way to Winter

The Autumn Journal

Wade Forbes

Spreading hope and scattering joy!

90 Days to Write Your Way to Winter

The Autumn Journal

Wade Forbes

Print: 978-1-7368912-2-3

Copyright ©2021 by Trembling Giant Marketing

Layout and Design by Trembling Giant Marketing, LLC.
www.TremblingGiantMarketing.com

This book is dedicated to all the people who started and wanted to finish. Now is your chance and there is no time to waste. Thank you to my beautiful family and friends for inspiring me to keep going.

The cover is dedicated to Alison Farmer for being in the moment with me when I asked what would be the best thing to appear on this autumn journal cover. We became 'summer camp friends' during COVID and I'm grateful for her inspiration and regular responses to my daily quotes.

Introduction

Whether we ask for it or not, the seasons change. A long time ago someone decided the actual date on the calendar that would begin the season, but for me, and for many of us, it's not quite that simple. In our minds, all it takes is one chilly August evening and we are ready for our fall wardrobe to fly out of our dressers. We imagine walking in the woods with the leaves as they change, the smell in the air, perhaps the various sporting events, and our favorite fall foods, too.

Fall arrived differently for me this year. With the new season came an accomplishment that I could not have begun to imagine this time last year, a complete set of seasonal journals. The advice that got me here was taught to me in third grade by my amazingly inspirational and kind teacher, Mrs. Stoy, at Anthiel Elementary School in Ewing, NJ. I was a creative kid who hovered from one assignment to another thinking that if I started a whole bunch of different things at once, I'd be done faster and could get back to my drawing. My not-very-thought-out plan quickly went south and I was overrun. Instead of getting ahead, I was always behind. I'd beat myself up. I'd say and think horrible things about myself. Then one day Mrs. Stoy said something so simple, it has stuck with me all these years. She said, "Wade, start one thing and just finish before moving to the next."

At the beginning of the pandemic, I told myself I was going to spread hope by drawing quotes on post-it notes every day. When those post-it notes covered my kitchen walls, I told myself I wanted to find a publisher to share my daily quotes and reflections. After speaking with the publisher, I self-published my winter journal in December 2020. As the year wore on, I maintained my daily habit of drawing and sharing quotes on social media and with colleagues I met. A spring journal was published, then a summer one, too. In order to truly bring Mrs. Stoy's advice and guidance to life, I had to complete the cycle and produce this autumn journal. Now that I'm finished, a journal for each season exists.

Start with small steps. What are you waiting for to finish? One season could be dedicated to an idea or a once unattainable goal. Another season may consist of stories you'd never shared or thought to write down. The season you decide to improve your self-talk might mean saying/writing kinder things for your soul to hear at the beginning or end of each day. Or, something unexpected happens and your journal is filled with how you processed this change, mourned the loss, found the path, made it right, and grew into a stronger person than you could have ever imagined.

Since I can remember, so many of my conversations seemed to start with all the difficult things that had happened or were happening. Recounting challenges, highlighting what someone else did, venting about struggles, listing woes, and even trying to one up each other on the awful things we experienced. Journeying through this pandemic, I learned that a short daily reflection guided me towards gratitude instantly. Instead of telling you all the things that went wrong, I was able to list all the things that went right. Did it mean that every day went perfectly? No. Did it mean that I was immune from frustrating situations? Nope. Did it give me a secret ability to succeed at everything on the first try? Not on your life. What it did do was make me feel less breakable. There was a time in my life where you could have broken me. You could have told me I wasn't good enough, that I didn't belong, that I was the one in the group who was not like the others and I would have crumbled. That person isn't here anymore.

Imagine what you could do if you felt less breakable. If you challenged yourself to finish? How would your life unfold if you wrote down the things that made you realize your purpose on the earth? Where would you begin to share your gifts? Who would you speak with first? Second? What would achieving your goals entail and what shifts would you need to make? I hope the illustrated quotes in this autumn journal edition take your mind to many places. That you won't put too many restraints on your thoughts as you open to a page that speaks to you.

Oh, and here's a bit of good news…these pages will wait for you even if you don't finish right away. By choosing to focus on yourself, you begin the journey towards mastering your thoughts, articulating your ambitions, and giving yourself a peace of mind that you may never have known. If you are familiar with the commitment to journaling, you're further along than me because I've only just begun.

Thank you for choosing hope, I am honored by any inspiration my illustrations give you. I hope that the small act of journaling takes you to a heightened state of mind, brings you closer to reaching the mental, emotional, and spiritual well-being you may have searched for, and you achieve things you never imagined were possible.

How This Journal is Meant to be Used

Did you know that journaling will:

- Lighten your load and give you a place for heavy thoughts?
- Allow you the time to study yourself, habits, goals, thoughts, and emotions?
- Reduce stress, expand your vocabulary, improve your emotional intelligence, and boost memory and comprehension?

Throw your ideas and desires onto the pages to help your reality take shape. Underneath each illustration is a space for you to doodle, dream, draw. Begin to imagine that, at the end, you won't be the same person you were when you started. Show kindness to yourself, and see what happens. You may even notice mistakes in the drawings in this journal which I left on purpose because no one is perfect. At the end, take a moment to reflect on what you've learned over the last 90 days and what you'd like to take with you into next winter.

THE WORLD DOESN'T REWARD PERFECTIONISTS. IT REWARDS THOSE WHO GET THINGS DONE.

Day 564. How we handle our mistakes is how we'll be remembered.

When the color version of my fall journal arrived, my good friend dropped off the boxes. We carried them inside and then we toasted to how much joy this project brings us.

A short while later, while sitting in my office, I held all four seasons in my hand and noticed something wrong on the spine of the latest journal. Instead of saying, "90 Days To Write Your Way to Winter: the Autumn Journal" it said "… Write Your Way To Autumn…" (again).

For a brief moment, I was not sure what to do. I entertained some disappointment, but then something really amazing happened. I fully embraced my mistake.

Some will say, "Wade, I would not have noticed unless you told me." To which I would reply, "There is a lesson in this though."

I've been drawing daily quotes for 18 months. You have seen proverbs from all over the world, quotes from famous people in history, and most importantly, reminders to go easy on yourself.

When your explore your journal, turn to these pages and you'll find:

- pg 20 - The world does not reward perfectionists. It rewards people who get things done.
- pg 106 - Shame says that because I am flawed, I am unacceptable. Grace says that though I am flawed, I am cherished.
- pg 136 - If you wished to be loved, show more of your faults than your virtues.
- pg 164 - To be creative, lose the fear of being wrong.
- pg 172 - Never confuse a single defeat with a final defeat.
- pg 176 - I will hold myself to a standard of grace.

As you can see, I've been preparing for this challenge from the very beginning. I could not have said or written this 563 days ago because I hadn't grown or reflected enough. Somewhere along the way I messed up because WE ARE SUPPOSED TO MESS UP.

So bring me your flaws. Put them down in a place that is safe so you can let yourself off the hook. Be exactly who you are publicly and privately otherwise it's going to catch up to you one way or the other.

I've already enhanced your journal a bit with a few extra pen strokes and now it's your turn to see who you really are.

-Wade

Concept by: A. Harrison

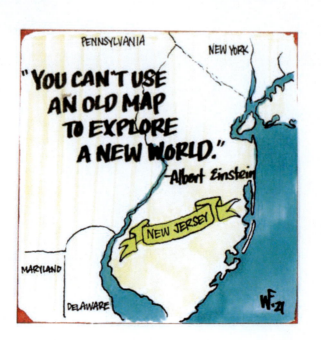

"MANY PEOPLE GO FISHING ALL THEIR LIVES WITHOUT KNOWING THAT IT IS NOT FISH THEY ARE AFTER." -Henry David Thoreau

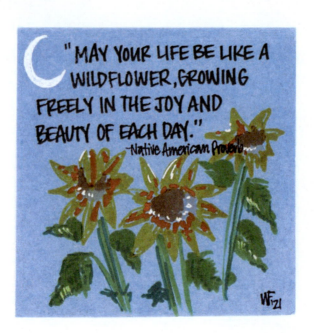

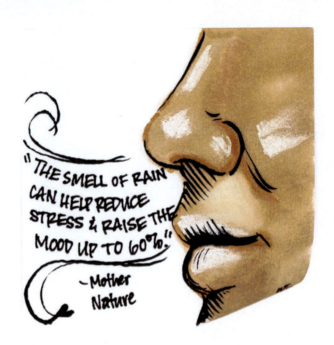

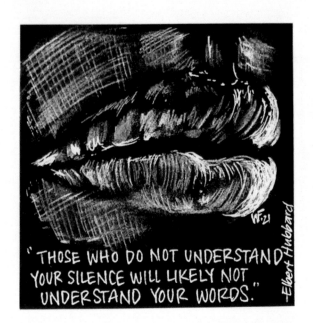

"THINK OF ALL THE BEAUTY STILL LEFT AROUND YOU AND BE HAPPY." -Anne Frank

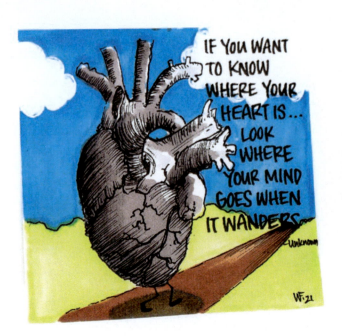

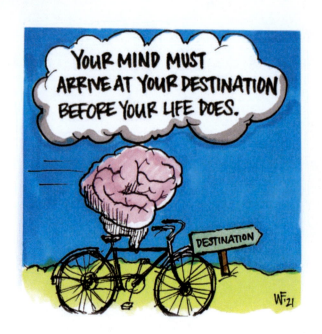

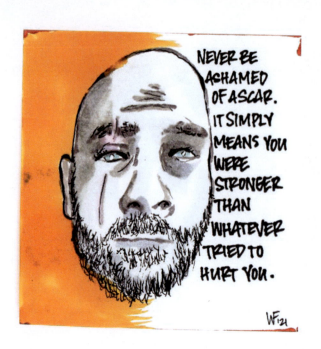

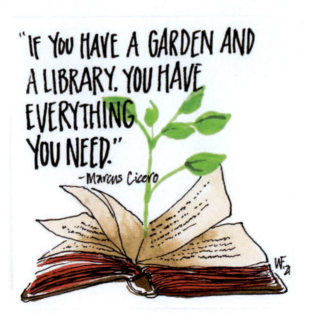

"WHEREVER THE ART OF MEDICINE IS LOVED, THERE IS ALSO A LOVE OF HUMANITY."
—Hippocrates

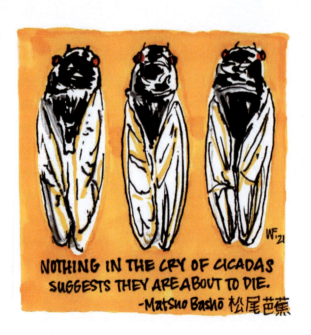

WORDS ARE THE FOG ONE HAS TO SEE THROUGH. —zen saying

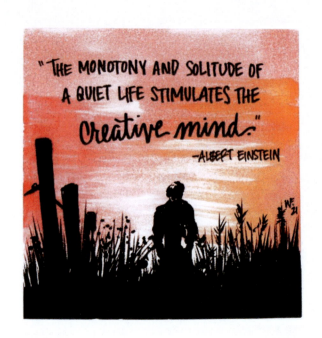

Now That Your Journal Is Full...

If you enjoyed this book, would you be so kind as to take a moment, go to www.drawforhope.com or Amazon, and leave a short review? Even if you only had time to go through a couple of pages you will be able to leave a review and, if you desire, go back later and add to it once you've had a chance to complete the book.

Your first impressions are very useful, so don't worry if you have only time now to review one or two elements.

Finally, note that books succeed by the kind, generous time readers take to leave honest reviews. This is how other readers learn about books that are most beneficial for them to buy. I thank you in advance for this very kind gesture of appreciation. It means the world to me.

How To Stay Connected To the RedTale Community:

To learn more about me and my illustration journey, and to hear other ways we are looking to spread hope to others, please visit www.redtale.com to join our mailing list. You can also follow me on Instagram @wadeforbes.

Acknowledgements

I'd like to thank Mrs. Stoy at Anthiel Elementary School in Ewing, NJ for teaching me back in the 1980s the importance of finishing what I started. My days are filled with so much more hope knowing that I can do anything now. Thank you to my friend Jeanette Passons for sharing how you cut the pages out of your journal to send notes to your son when he goes to school. Thank you to my pastor Tiffany Patterson for using these journals to overcome writer's block so you can say something inspiring and important that needs to be said. Thank you to Lydia Vickery for helping me to amplify the power these journals can have and for helping me organize my work. Thank you to Rich Austin and Emily Conley at Trembling Giant Marketing for bringing these pages and my images to life. Without you, I'd be surrounded by post-it notes and wishing I knew more ways to share. Thank you to Kristin Cook for taking my quotes and weaving them into your impressive and timely wellness work at Bluebird Yoga and Wellness. Your ability to take a quote and leverage the theme so that others can find peace is an act of pure beauty and grace. Thank you to Freedom Chiropractic and Rehab, Blackbird CrossFit, PinItUp Acupuncture, Therapeutic Needs, and Market Tavern for selling my journals to the community. I am grateful for your support and assistance in spreading hope.

To those of you who purchased the other seasonal journals, you continue to light a spark inside me that says over and over again hope can win. On days I feel a little discouraged and the doubt devil is winning, I smile knowing that there are more of us spreading hope than before. Together, we can start those long overdue projects, conversations, and activities that keep the light on inside ourselves and others. And finally, thank you to my wife Megan Forbes for meeting me where I am each day. Being married to an artist who is constantly thinking about something is not easy and you never know who you're going to get when you walk into our office each day. I'm grateful you continue to brighten up my world and lead our family during the most unique time in our lives (so far).